I AM
ECHAD

AM ISRAEL CHAI

ERETZ
ISRAEL
ISRAEL

BELONGING
BELONGING

ROOM'S

BELONGING

AM ISRAEL CHAI

AM
ECHAD

JER-USA-LEM

JER LEM USA
USA JER USA
JER USA LEM
LEM USA LEM
USA JER USA

FRIENDSHIP

FRIENDSHIP

Be Brave
AM ISAEL

FRIENDSHIP

LOYALTY

AM
ISRAEL
CHAI

AM
ISRAEL
CHAI

IDF
IDF

AM ISRAEL CHAI
לָנֶצַח

AM ISRAEL CHAI

ISRAEL CHAI

I LOVE
ISRAEL

I LOVE
ISRAEL

SHEMA

SHEMA
YISRAEL
SHEMA YISRAEL

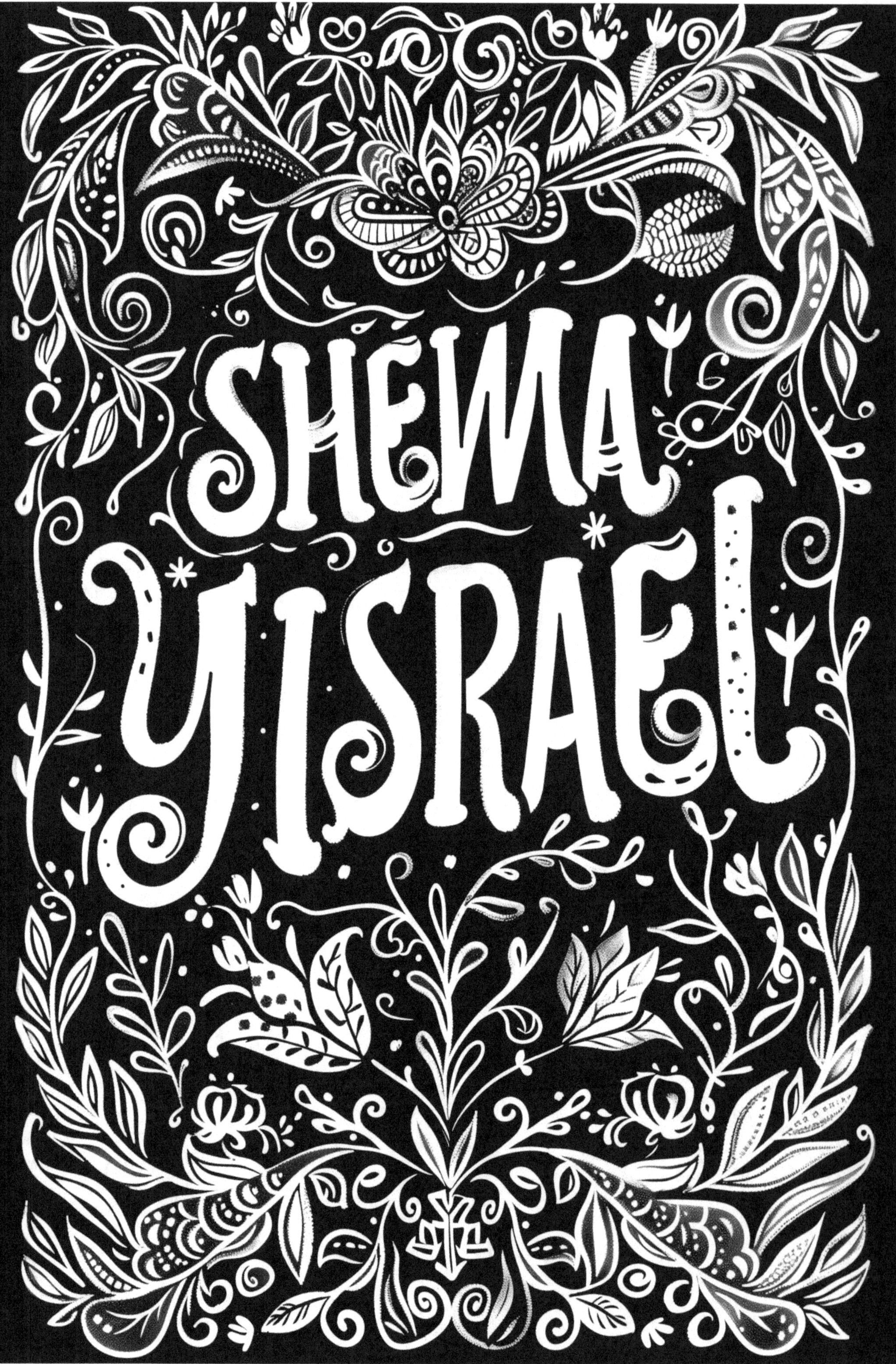

SHEMA
YISRAEL

ED
4

TODA
TODA

NEFESH
YEHUDI

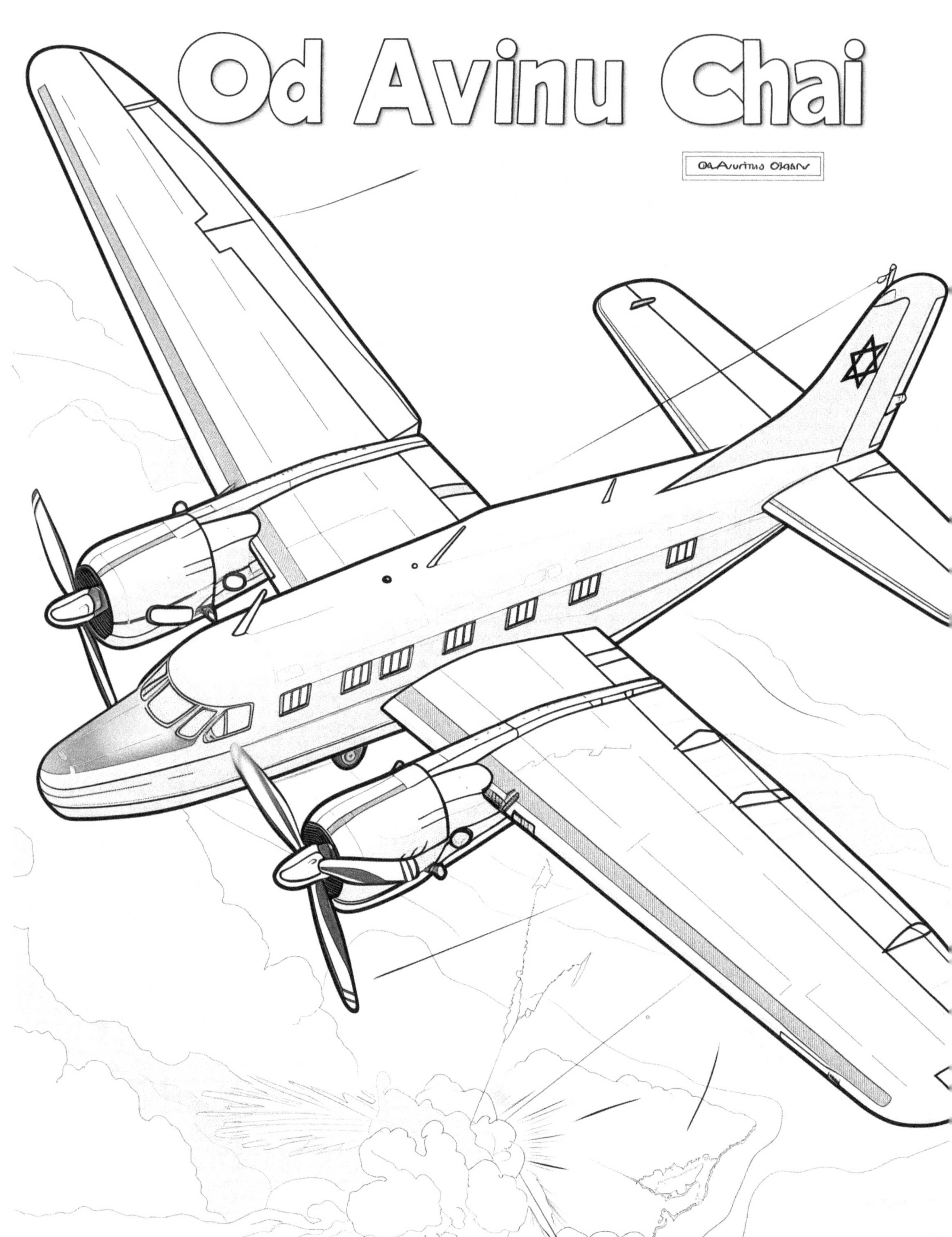
Od Avinu Chai

ERETZ
ISRAEL

AM ISRAEL
CHAI

עם ישראל חי

ISRAEL CHAAI
AM ISRAEL
AM CHAI

TRENDS

AL TIRA
YISRAEL

Od Avinu
Chai

ISRAEL

Unity